MW00571113

FOR THE BEST GRANDPARENT IN THE WORLD

summersdale

FOR THE BEST GRANDPARENT IN THE WORLD

Text compiled by Elanor Clarke

Summersdale Publishers Ltd
46 West Street
Chichester
West Sussex
PO19 1RP
UK

www.summersdale.com

Printed and bound in the Czech Republic

ISBN: 978-1-84953-674-5

Substantial discounts on bulk quantities of Summersdale books are available to corporations, professional associations and other organisations. For details contact Nicky Douglas by telephone: +44 (0) 1243 756902, fax: +44 (0) 1243 786300 or email: nicky@summersdale.com.

TO..

FROM...

GRANDPARENTS
ARE THERE TO HELP
THE CHILD GET INTO
MISCHIEF THEY HAVEN'T
THOUGHT OF YET.

Gene Perret

IN TIME OF TEST, FAMILY IS BEST.

Burmese proverb

ONE ADVANTAGE
OF GROWING OLDER IS
THAT YOU CAN STAND
FOR MORE AND FALL
FOR LESS.

Monta Crane

NO MATTER HOW MANY
GRANDCHILDREN YOU
MAY HAVE, EACH ONE
HOLDS A SPECIAL PLACE
IN YOUR HEART.

Alvaretta Roberts

MY GRANDFATHER WAS THE MOST SELFLESS PERSON I KNOW.

Cat Dugdale

WE ALL GROW UP WITH
THE WEIGHT OF HISTORY
ON US. OUR ANCESTORS
DWELL IN THE ATTICS
OF OUR BRAINS.

Shirley Abbott

WHEN YOU LOOK AT YOUR
LIFE, THE GREATEST
HAPPINESSES ARE
FAMILY HAPPINESSES.

Joyce Brothers

AN OUNCE OF BLOOD IS WORTH MORE THAN A POUND OF FRIENDSHIP.

Spanish proverb

THERE IS NO CURE FOR LAZINESS BUT A LARGE FAMILY HELPS.

Herbert Prochnow

TALKING TO YOU HELPS ME LEARN WHO I AM

OTHER THINGS MAY CHANGE US, BUT WE START AND END WITH FAMILY.

Anthony Brandt

IF NOTHING IS GOING WELL, CALL YOUR GRANDMOTHER.

Italian proverb

AS WE SEEK TO
STRENGTHEN THE
ENDURING VALUES
OF THE FAMILY, IT IS
APPROPRIATE THAT
WE HONOUR OUR
GRANDPARENTS.

Jimmy Carter

GRANDMA... MADE YOU
FEEL SHE HAD BEEN
WAITING TO SEE JUST
YOU ALL DAY AND NOW
THE DAY WAS COMPLETE.

Marcy DeMaree

THEY GIVE
UNCONDITIONAL LOVE,
KINDNESS, PATIENCE,
HUMOUR, COMFORT,
LESSONS IN LIFE. AND,
MOST IMPORTANTLY,
COOKIES.

Rudy Giuliani on grandparents

ON THE SEVENTH
DAY GOD RESTED. HIS
GRANDCHILDREN MUST
HAVE BEEN OUT
OF TOWN.

Gene Perret

LOVE IS THE GREATEST GIFT THAT ONE GENERATION CAN LEAVE TO ANOTHER.

Richard Garnett

THE SIMPLEST TOY,
ONE WHICH EVEN THE
YOUNGEST CHILD CAN
OPERATE, IS CALLED
A GRANDPARENT.

Sam Levenson

BLESSED BE THE TIES THAT BIND GENERATIONS.

Anonymous

THEY SAY THAT GENES
SKIP GENERATIONS.
MAYBE THAT'S WHY
GRANDPARENTS FIND
THEIR GRANDCHILDREN
SO LIKEABLE.

Joan McIntosh

YOU ALWAYS
MAKE US FEEL
LOVED

FAMILY IS THE MOST IMPORTANT THING IN THE WORLD.

Diana, Princess of Wales

A GRANDFATHER IS SOMEONE YOU CAN LOOK UP TO NO MATTER HOW TALL YOU GROW.

Anonymous

GRANDPARENTS, LIKE
HEROES, ARE AS
NECESSARY TO A CHILD'S
GROWTH AS VITAMINS.

Joyce Allston

THE IDEA THAT NO ONE
IS PERFECT IS A VIEW
MOST COMMONLY HELD
BY PEOPLE WITH NO
GRANDCHILDREN.

Doug Larson

NOBODY CAN DO FOR
LITTLE CHILDREN WHAT
GRANDPARENTS DO.
GRANDPARENTS SORT
OF SPRINKLE STARDUST
OVER THE LIVES OF
LITTLE CHILDREN.

Alex Haley

SOMETIMES OUR GRANDMAS AND GRANDPAS ARE LIKE GRAND-ANGELS.

Lexie Saige

WHEN GRANDPARENTS
ENTER THE DOOR,
DISCIPLINE FLIES OUT
THE WINDOW.

Ogden Nash

CHILDREN WILL NOT
REMEMBER YOU FOR
THE MATERIAL THINGS
YOU PROVIDED, BUT FOR
THE FEELING THAT YOU
CHERISHED THEM.

Richard L. Evans

SOMETIMES YOU WILL
NEVER KNOW THE VALUE
OF A MOMENT UNTIL IT
BECOMES A MEMORY.

Dr Seuss

YOU ARE NEVER TOO
OLD TO SET ANOTHER
GOAL OR TO DREAM
A NEW DREAM.

C. S. Lewis

IT IS AS GRANDMOTHERS
THAT OUR MOTHERS COME
INTO THE FULLNESS OF
THEIR GRACE.

Christopher Morley

WRINKLES SHOULD MERELY INDICATE WHERE SMILES HAVE BEEN.

Mark Twain

YOU GIVE THE
BEST HUGS

GRANDMOTHERS
ARE JUST ANTIQUE
LITTLE GIRLS.

Anonymous

PERFECT LOVE SOMETIMES DOES NOT COME UNTIL THE FIRST GRANDCHILD.

Welsh proverb

A CHILD NEEDS A
GRANDPARENT, ANYBODY'S
GRANDPARENT, TO GROW
A LITTLE MORE SECURELY
INTO AN UNFAMILIAR
WORLD.

Charles and Ann Morse

A HOUSE NEEDS A GRANDMA IN IT.

Louisa May Alcott

I ALWAYS GIVE MY
GRANDKIDS A COUPLE
OF QUARTERS WHEN
THEY GO HOME. IT'S
A BARGAIN.

Gene Perret

NEVER HAVE CHILDREN, ONLY GRANDCHILDREN.

Gore Vidal

WE SHOULD ALL HAVE
ONE PERSON WHO KNOWS
HOW TO BLESS US
DESPITE THE EVIDENCE.
GRANDMOTHER WAS
THAT PERSON.

Phyllis Theroux

IT IS ONE OF NATURE'S
WAYS THAT WE OFTEN
FEEL CLOSER TO DISTANT
GENERATIONS THAN TO THE
GENERATION IMMEDIATELY
PRECEDING US.

Igor Stravinsky

BEING GRANDPARENTS
SUFFICIENTLY
REMOVES US FROM THE
RESPONSIBILITIES SO THAT
WE CAN BE FRIENDS.

Allan Frome

IT WOULD BE MORE
HONOURABLE TO
OUR DISTINGUISHED
ANCESTORS TO PRAISE
THEM IN WORDS LESS,
BUT IN DEEDS TO
IMITATE THEM MORE.

Horace Mann

GRANDCHILDREN
ARE THE DOTS THAT
CONNECT THE LINES
FROM GENERATION TO
GENERATION.

Lois Wyse

FAMILY — THAT DEAR
OCTOPUS FROM WHOSE
TENTACLES WE NEVER
QUITE ESCAPE, NOR, IN
OUR INNERMOST HEARTS,
EVER QUITE WISH TO.

Dodie Smith

ELEPHANTS AND
GRANDCHILDREN
NEVER FORGET.

Andy Rooney

HOLDING A
GREAT-GRANDCHILD
MAKES GETTING OLD
WORTHWHILE.

Evalyn Rikkers

YOU ALWAYS
KNOW THE RIGHT
THING TO SAY

UNCLES AND AUNTS,
AND COUSINS, ARE
ALL VERY WELL, AND
FATHERS AND MOTHERS
ARE NOT TO BE DESPISED;
BUT A GRANDMOTHER,
AT HOLIDAY TIME, IS
WORTH THEM ALL.

Fanny Fern

THE REASON
GRANDCHILDREN AND
GRANDPARENTS GET
ALONG SO WELL IS THAT
THEY BOTH SHARE THE
SAME ENEMY.

Sam Levenson

EVERYONE NEEDS TO
HAVE ACCESS BOTH TO
GRANDPARENTS AND
GRANDCHILDREN IN
ORDER TO BE A FULL
HUMAN BEING.

Margaret Mead

TO BECOME A
GRANDPARENT IS TO
ENJOY ONE OF THE
FEW PLEASURES IN
LIFE FOR WHICH THE
CONSEQUENCES HAVE
ALREADY BEEN PAID.

Robert Brault

A GRANDFATHER IS SOMEONE WITH SILVER IN HIS HAIR AND GOLD IN HIS HEART.

Anonymous

IF BECOMING A
GRANDMOTHER WAS ONLY
A MATTER OF CHOICE, I
SHOULD ADVISE EVERY
ONE OF YOU STRAIGHT
AWAY TO BECOME ONE.
THERE IS NO FUN FOR
OLD PEOPLE LIKE IT!

Hannah Whitall Smith

I LOVED THEIR HOME.
EVERYTHING SMELLED
OLDER, WORN BUT SAFE;
THE FOOD AROMA HAD
BAKED ITSELF INTO
THE FURNITURE.

Susan Strasberg on her
grandparents' home

GRANDFATHERS ARE FOR LOVING AND FIXING THINGS.

Anonymous

YOU DO NOT REALLY
UNDERSTAND SOMETHING
UNLESS YOU CAN
EXPLAIN IT TO YOUR
GRANDMOTHER.

Proverb

AN HOUR WITH YOUR
GRANDCHILDREN CAN
MAKE YOU FEEL YOUNG
AGAIN. ANYTHING
LONGER THAN THAT,
AND YOU START TO
AGE QUICKLY.

Gene Perret

THE PERFECT GRANDDAD
IS UNAFRAID OF BIG DOGS
AND FIERCE STORMS BUT
ABSOLUTELY TERRIFIED
OF THE WORD 'BOO'.

Robert Brault

A GRANDPARENT IS OLD ON THE OUTSIDE BUT YOUNG ON THE INSIDE.

Anonymous

BAKING WITH
YOU IS THE
BEST FUN!

ONE OF THE MOST
POWERFUL HANDCLASPS
IS THAT OF A NEW
GRANDBABY AROUND
THE FINGER OF A
GRANDFATHER.

Joy Hargrove

EVERY GENERATION
REVOLTS AGAINST ITS
FATHERS AND MAKES
FRIENDS WITH ITS
GRANDFATHERS.

Lewis Mumford

A GRANDMOTHER IS
A SAFE HAVEN.

Suzette Haden Elgin

IT'S AMAZING HOW
GRANDPARENTS SEEM
SO YOUNG ONCE YOU
BECOME ONE.

Anonymous

SURELY, TWO OF THE
MOST SATISFYING
EXPERIENCES IN LIFE
MUST BE THOSE OF
BEING A GRANDCHILD
OR A GRANDPARENT.

Donald A. Norberg

MOST GRANDMAS
HAVE A TOUCH OF
THE SCALLYWAG.

Helen Thomson

YOU'VE GOT TO DO YOUR
OWN GROWING, NO
MATTER HOW TALL YOUR
GRANDFATHER WAS.

Irish proverb

A GRANDMOTHER PRETENDS SHE DOESN'T KNOW WHO YOU ARE ON HALLOWEEN.

Erma Bombeck

IT IS INTO US THAT THE
LIVES OF GRANDPARENTS
HAVE GONE. IT IS IN US
THAT THEIR HISTORY
BECOMES A FUTURE.

Charles and Ann Morse

WITH YOUR
GRANDPARENTS YOU HAVE
A FEELING THAT YOU CAN
SAY ANYTHING... YOU CAN
DO ANYTHING, AND THEY
WILL SUPPORT YOU.

Novak Djokovic

GRANDMOTHER — A WONDERFUL MOTHER WITH LOTS OF PRACTICE.

Anonymous

A GRANDAM'S NAME IS LITTLE LESS IN LOVE THAN IS THE DOTING TITLE OF A MOTHER.

William Shakespeare

BY THE TIME THE
YOUNGEST CHILDREN
HAVE LEARNED TO KEEP
THE HOUSE TIDY, THE
OLDEST GRANDCHILDREN...
TEAR IT TO PIECES.

Christopher Morley

MY GRANDFATHER WAS
A WONDERFUL ROLE
MODEL. THROUGH HIM
I GOT TO KNOW THE
GENTLE SIDE OF MEN.

Sarah Long

YOU KNOW JUST
WHAT TO SAY TO
MAKE MUM AND
DAD CHANGE
THEIR MINDS

OUR GRANDCHILDREN
ACCEPT US FOR
OURSELVES... NOT OUR
PARENTS, SIBLINGS,
SPOUSES, FRIENDS — AND
HARDLY EVER OUR OWN
GROWN CHILDREN.

Ruth Goode

TO SHOW A CHILD
WHAT HAS ONCE
DELIGHTED YOU, TO FIND
THE CHILD'S DELIGHT
ADDED TO YOUR OWN...
IS HAPPINESS.

J. B. Priestley

IT'S SO IMPORTANT TO
GIVE YOUR CHILDREN
AND GRANDCHILDREN
INSPIRATION... TEACH
THEM TO NOTICE, TO
PAY ATTENTION, TO
APPRECIATE.

Irina Baronova

LEARNING IS EVER
IN THE FRESHNESS
OF ITS YOUTH, EVEN
FOR THE OLD.

Aeschylus

TO KEEP THE HEART
UNWRINKLED, TO BE
HOPEFUL, KINDLY,
CHEERFUL, REVERENT
— THAT IS TO TRIUMPH
OVER OLD AGE.

Thomas Bailey Aldrich

WHEN YOU HAVE A GRANDCHILD, YOU HAVE TWO CHILDREN.

Jewish proverb

FAMILY FACES
ARE MAGIC MIRRORS.
LOOKING AT PEOPLE WHO
BELONG TO US, WE SEE
THE PAST, PRESENT
AND FUTURE.

Gail Lumet Buckley

AH WELL, PERHAPS ONE
HAS TO BE VERY OLD
BEFORE ONE LEARNS
HOW TO BE AMUSED
RATHER THAN SHOCKED.

Pearl S. Buck

A PEOPLE WITHOUT HISTORY IS LIKE WIND ON THE BUFFALO GRASS.

Sioux proverb

YOU DON'T CHOOSE
YOUR FAMILY. THEY ARE
GOD'S GIFT TO YOU, AS
YOU ARE TO THEM.

Desmond Tutu

THOSE WHO HAVE NO GRANDPARENTS LOSE VERY MUCH.

Spanish proverb

MY GRANDFATHER WAS
A GIANT OF A MAN...
WHEN HE WALKED,
THE EARTH SHOOK.

Eth Clifford

GRANDPARENTS
SHOULD PLAY THE SAME
ROLE IN THE FAMILY AS
AN ELDER STATESMAN IN
THE GOVERNMENT OF
A COUNTRY.

Geoff Dench

NO SPRING NOR SUMMER
BEAUTY HATH SUCH
GRACE AS I HAVE SEEN
IN ONE AUTUMNAL FACE.

John Donne

GRANDMOTHERS NEVER RUN OUT OF HUGS OR COOKIES.

Anonymous

JUST ABOUT THE
TIME A WOMAN THINKS
HER WORK IS DONE,
SHE BECOMES A
GRANDMOTHER.

Edward H. Dreschnack

YOU KNOW THE
BEST GAMES

I WISH I HAD
THE ENERGY THAT
MY GRANDCHILDREN
HAVE — IF ONLY FOR
SELF-DEFENCE.

Gene Perret

WE FIND DELIGHT
IN THE BEAUTY AND
HAPPINESS OF CHILDREN
THAT MAKES THE HEART
TOO BIG FOR THE BODY.

Ralph Waldo Emerson

WHAT A WONDERFUL
CONTRIBUTION OUR
GRANDMOTHERS
AND GRANDFATHERS
CAN MAKE IF THEY
WILL SHARE... THEIR
TESTIMONIES.

Vaughn J. Featherstone

BLOOD IS A DESTINY. ONE'S
GENIUS DESCENDS IN
THE STREAM FROM LONG
LINES OF ANCESTRY.

Amos Bronson Alcott

IF YOU WOULD CIVILISE
A MAN, BEGIN WITH HIS
GRANDMOTHER.

Victor Hugo

LIFE IS A COUNTRY
THAT THE OLD HAVE
SEEN, AND LIVED IN.
THOSE WHO HAVE TO
TRAVEL THROUGH IT
CAN ONLY LEARN THE
WAY FROM THEM.

Joseph Joubert

SOUP SIMMERING,
MUSIC OF IDLE GOSSIP,
YAMMERING KIDS,
DOMESTIC CHAOS —
LONG ADJUSTED TO THIS
ROLLING SCENE, YOU
SHOW THEM YOUR
LOFTY CALM.

Gottfried Keller

YOUNG PEOPLE NEED
SOMETHING STABLE TO
HANG ON TO... MOST OF
ALL, THEY NEED WHAT
GRANDPARENTS CAN
GIVE THEM.

Jay Kesler

GRANDMOTHERS ARE THE VOICES OF THE PAST AND ROLE MODELS OF THE PRESENT.

Anonymous

GRANDMOTHERS
OPEN THE DOORS TO
THE FUTURE.

Helen Ketchum

IF GRANDMAS HADN'T
EXISTED, KIDS WOULD
HAVE INEVITABLY
INVENTED THEM.

Arthur Kornhaber

WHEN YOU BECOME
A GRANDPARENT...
YOU START TO ACT ALL
GOOFY AND DO THINGS
YOU NEVER THOUGHT
YOU'D DO.

Mike Krzyzewski

YOU MAKE EVEN THE RAINIEST DAY A FUN DAY

WE MUST ACT AS
THE ELDERS OF THE
TRIBE... PRESERVING
THE PRECIOUS COMPACT
BETWEEN THE
GENERATIONS.

Maggie Kuhn

NO ONE WHO HAS
NOT KNOWN THAT
INESTIMABLE PRIVILEGE
CAN POSSIBLY REALISE
WHAT GOOD FORTUNE
IT IS.

Suzanne La Follette on growing up
with grandparents

IT'S IMPOSSIBLE
FOR A GRANDMOTHER
TO UNDERSTAND THAT
FEW PEOPLE... WILL
FIND HER GRANDCHILD
AS ENDEARING AS
SHE DOES.

Janet Lanese

FEW THINGS ARE MORE DELIGHTFUL THAN GRANDCHILDREN FIGHTING OVER YOUR LAP.

Doug Larson

TO US, FAMILY MEANS
PUTTING YOUR ARMS
AROUND EACH OTHER
AND BEING THERE.

Barbara Bush

SOMETHING MAGICAL HAPPENS WHEN PARENTS TURN INTO GRANDPARENTS.

Paul Linden

POSTERITY IS THE PATRIOTIC NAME FOR GRANDCHILDREN.

Art Linkletter

THE ONLY ROCK I KNOW
THAT STAYS STEADY,
THE ONLY INSTITUTION
I KNOW THAT WORKS IS
THE FAMILY.

Lee Iacocca

WHEN IT SEEMS
THE WORLD CAN'T
UNDERSTAND, YOUR
GRANDMOTHER'S THERE
TO HOLD YOUR HAND.

Joyce K. Allen Logan

THERE IS A FOUNTAIN
OF YOUTH: IT IS YOUR
MIND, YOUR TALENTS,
THE CREATIVITY YOU
BRING TO YOUR LIFE
AND THE LIVES OF THE
PEOPLE YOU LOVE.

Sophia Loren

[IT IS] OUR LAST CHANCE TO ACT LIKE A KID WITHOUT BEING ACCUSED OF BEING IN OUR SECOND CHILDHOOD.

Janet Lanese on being a grandmother

IN A SHORT SPACE
THE GENERATIONS OF
LIVING CREATURES ARE
CHANGED AND, LIKE
RUNNERS, PASS ON THE
TORCH OF LIFE.

Lucretius

IN EVERY CONCEIVABLE
MANNER, THE FAMILY
IS LINK TO OUR PAST,
BRIDGE TO OUR FUTURE.

Alex Haley

IN ORDER NOT TO
INFLUENCE A CHILD,
ONE MUST BE CAREFUL
NOT TO BE THAT
CHILD'S PARENT OR
GRANDPARENT.

Don Marquis

A GARDEN OF
LOVE GROWS IN A
GRANDMOTHER'S HEART.

Anonymous

JUST AS A FATHER
FEELS IT IS ALL
ENDING... IN MIDLIFE,
DAD MAY EXPERIENCE HIS
SECOND 'FATHERHOOD' AS
A GRANDPARENT.

Alvin Francis Poussaint

EVERYTHING'S BETTER WHEN YOU'RE AROUND

EVEN YOUNG
GRANDPARENTS SEEM
ENORMOUSLY OLD TO A
SMALL CHILD, ALTHOUGH
THE CHILD MAY POLITELY
DENY IT.

Alison Judson Ryerson

GOOD OLD GRANDSIRE...
WE SHALL BE JOYFUL
OF THY COMPANY.

William Shakespeare

SOME OF THE WORLD'S BEST EDUCATORS ARE GRANDPARENTS.

Charles W. Shedd

THE IMPORTANT THING...
IS NOT HOW MANY YEARS
IN YOUR LIFE, BUT HOW
MUCH LIFE IN YOUR
YEARS!

Edward Stieglitz

IT'S NOT THAT AGE
BRINGS CHILDHOOD BACK
AGAIN. AGE MERELY
SHOWS WHAT CHILDREN
WE REMAIN.

Johann Wolfgang von Goethe

YOU ARE THE SUN, GRANDMA, YOU ARE THE SUN IN MY LIFE.

Kitty Tsui

CALL IT A TRIBE, CALL
IT A FAMILY. WHATEVER
YOU CALL IT, WHOEVER
YOU ARE, YOU NEED ONE.

Jane Howard

WE HAVE BECOME
A GRANDMOTHER.

Margaret Thatcher

THE FAMILY IS ONE OF NATURE'S MASTERPIECES.

George Santayana

AS A CHILD I KNEW
ALMOST NOTHING,
NOTHING BEYOND WHAT
I HAD PICKED UP IN MY
GRANDMOTHER'S HOUSE.

V. S. Naipaul

IF YOU KNOW HIS FATHER AND GRANDFATHER, DON'T WORRY ABOUT HIS SON.

African proverb

THE BEST BABYSITTERS...
ARE THE BABY'S GRANDPARENTS... WHICH IS WHY MOST GRANDPARENTS FLEE TO FLORIDA.

Dave Barry

MY GRANDMOTHER
WOULD SAY... 'MAKE
SURE YOU REMAIN THAT
SOUTHERN GENTLEMAN
THAT I'VE TAUGHT
YOU TO BE.'

Jamie Foxx

WHAT WE OWE OUR PARENTS IS THE BILL PRESENTED TO US BY OUR CHILDREN.

Nancy Friday

YOUR HOUSE IS LIKE A TREASURE CHEST, FULL OF AMAZING THINGS

GRANDCHILDREN ARE GOD'S WAY OF COMPENSATING US FOR GROWING OLD.

Mary H. Waldrip

IT IS, I SUPPOSE,
THE BUSINESS OF
GRANDPARENTS TO
CREATE MEMORIES
AND THE RELATIVE OF
MEMORIES: TRADITIONS.

Ellen Goodman

REJOICE WITH YOUR FAMILY IN THE BEAUTIFUL LAND OF LIFE!

Albert Einstein

WHAT GREATER THING
IS THERE FOR HUMAN
SOULS THAN TO FEEL
THAT THEY ARE JOINED
FOR LIFE — TO BE
WITH EACH OTHER IN
SILENT UNSPEAKABLE
MEMORIES.

George Eliot

GRANDCHILDREN DON'T
STAY YOUNG FOREVER,
WHICH IS GOOD BECAUSE
POP-POPS HAVE ONLY SO
MANY HORSEY RIDES
IN THEM.

Gene Perret

THE HAPPIEST MOMENTS OF MY LIFE HAVE BEEN THE FEW WHICH I HAVE PASSED... IN THE BOSOM OF MY FAMILY.

Thomas Jefferson

ONE OF LIFE'S GREATEST
MYSTERIES IS HOW THE
BOY WHO WASN'T GOOD
ENOUGH TO MARRY
YOUR DAUGHTER CAN
BE THE FATHER OF THE
SMARTEST GRANDCHILD
IN THE WORLD.

Jewish proverb

THE MORE YOU LOVE,
THE MORE LOVE YOU
HAVE TO GIVE. IT'S THE
ONLY FEELING WE HAVE
WHICH IS INFINITE.

Christina Westover

A HAPPY FAMILY IS BUT AN EARLIER HEAVEN.

George Bernard Shaw

IF GOD HAD INTENDED US
TO FOLLOW RECIPES, HE
WOULDN'T HAVE GIVEN
US GRANDMOTHERS.

Linda Henley

MY GRANDFATHER
ALWAYS SAID THAT
LIVING IS LIKE LICKING
HONEY OFF A THORN.

Louis Adamic

THE HOUSE WITH AN OLD GRANDPARENT HARBOURS A JEWEL.

Chinese proverb

GROWING OLD IS MANDATORY; GROWING UP IS OPTIONAL.

Carroll Bryant

THE YEARS TEACH
MUCH WHICH THE DAYS
NEVER KNOW.

Ralph Waldo Emerson

EVERYONE IS THE AGE OF THEIR HEART.

Guatemalan proverb

THERE IS NO OLD AGE.
THERE IS, AS THERE
ALWAYS WAS, JUST YOU.

Carol Grace